EASTER
CUT AND PASTE
For Kids, Toddlers
Preschool

What picture comes next ?

1 - Color the Eggs
2 - Put the Eggs in the Basket.

Help the bunny juggle the Eggs

What picture comes next ?

1 - Cut The shapes in the bottom of the page
2 - Find the shape in the image
3 - Paste the shape on the right position.

Cut an paste the Easter Words .

1 - Cut an paste the Easter Words .
2 - Color the rabbit .

Addition Game .
Cut and Paste the right answers

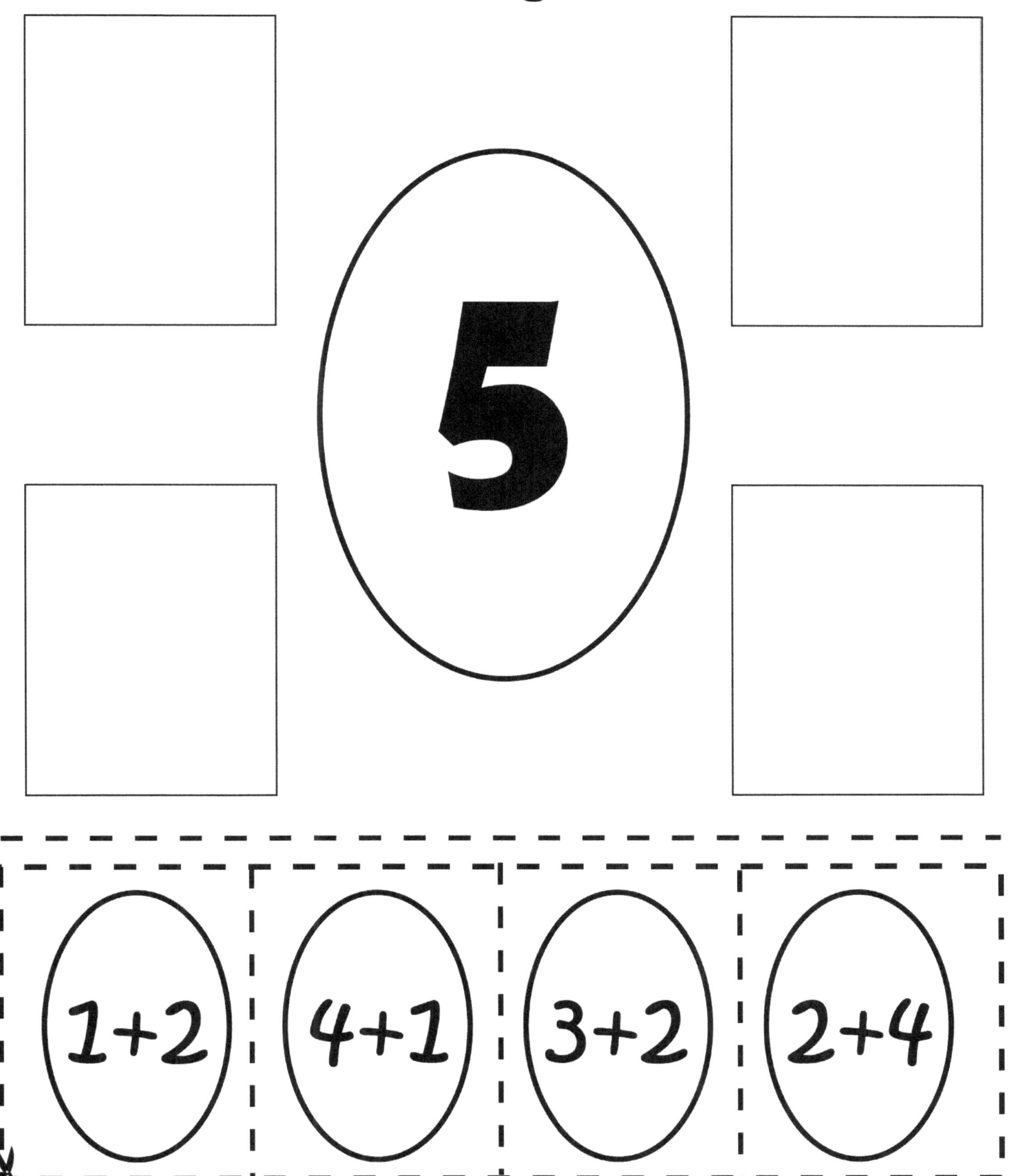

Addition Game .
Cut and Paste the right answers

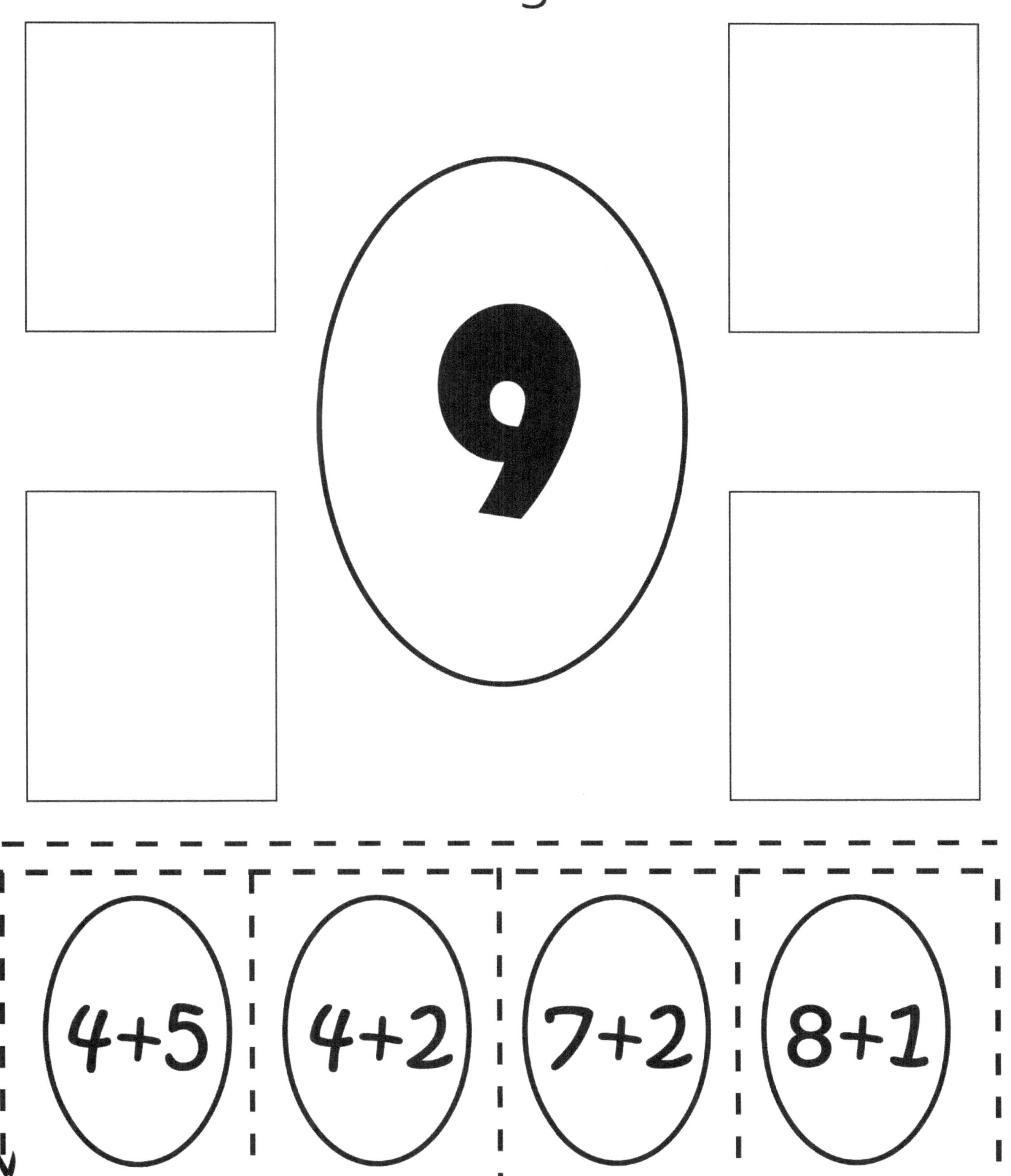

Addition Game .
Cut and Paste the right answers

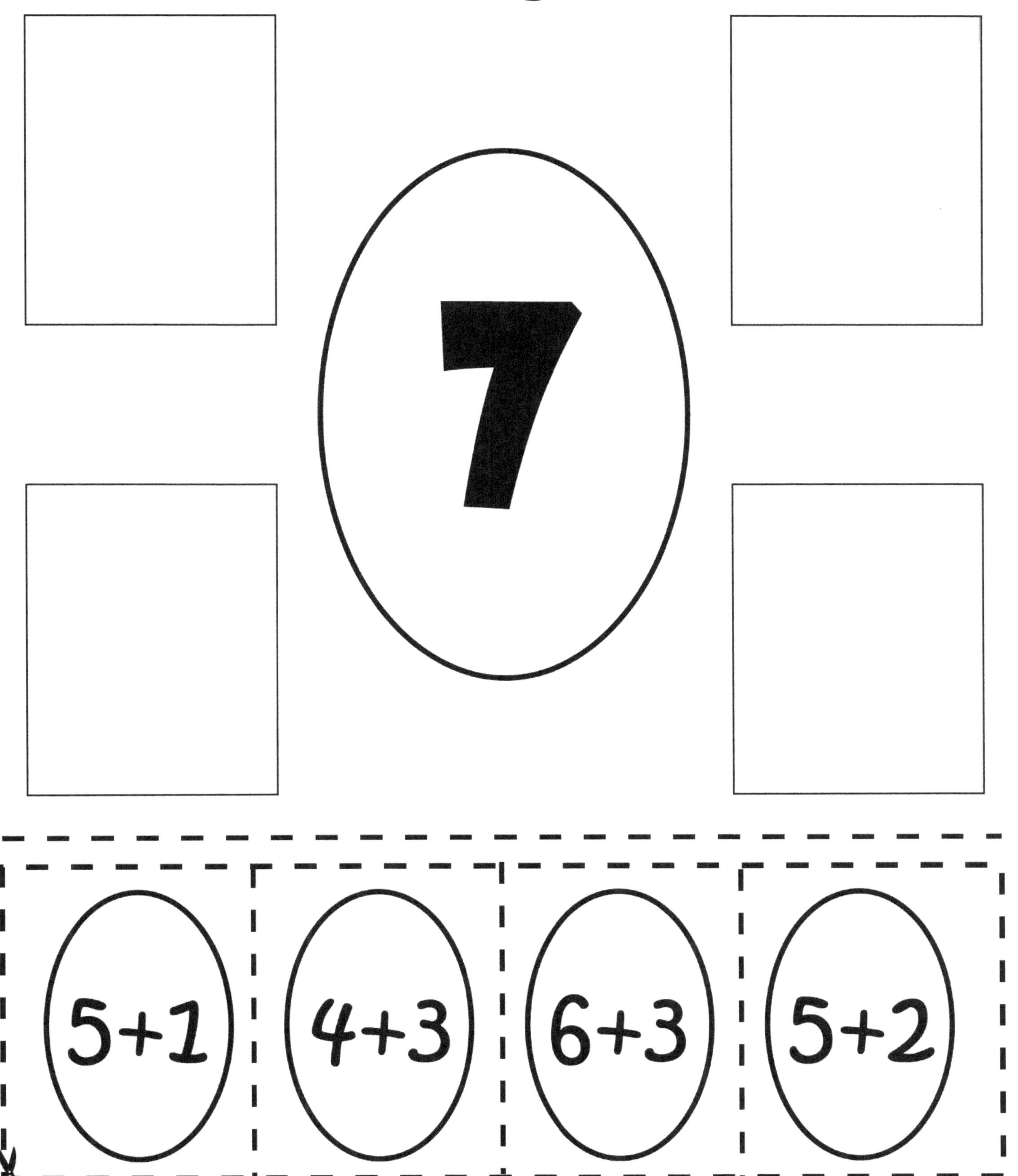

Cut and the paste in the right position

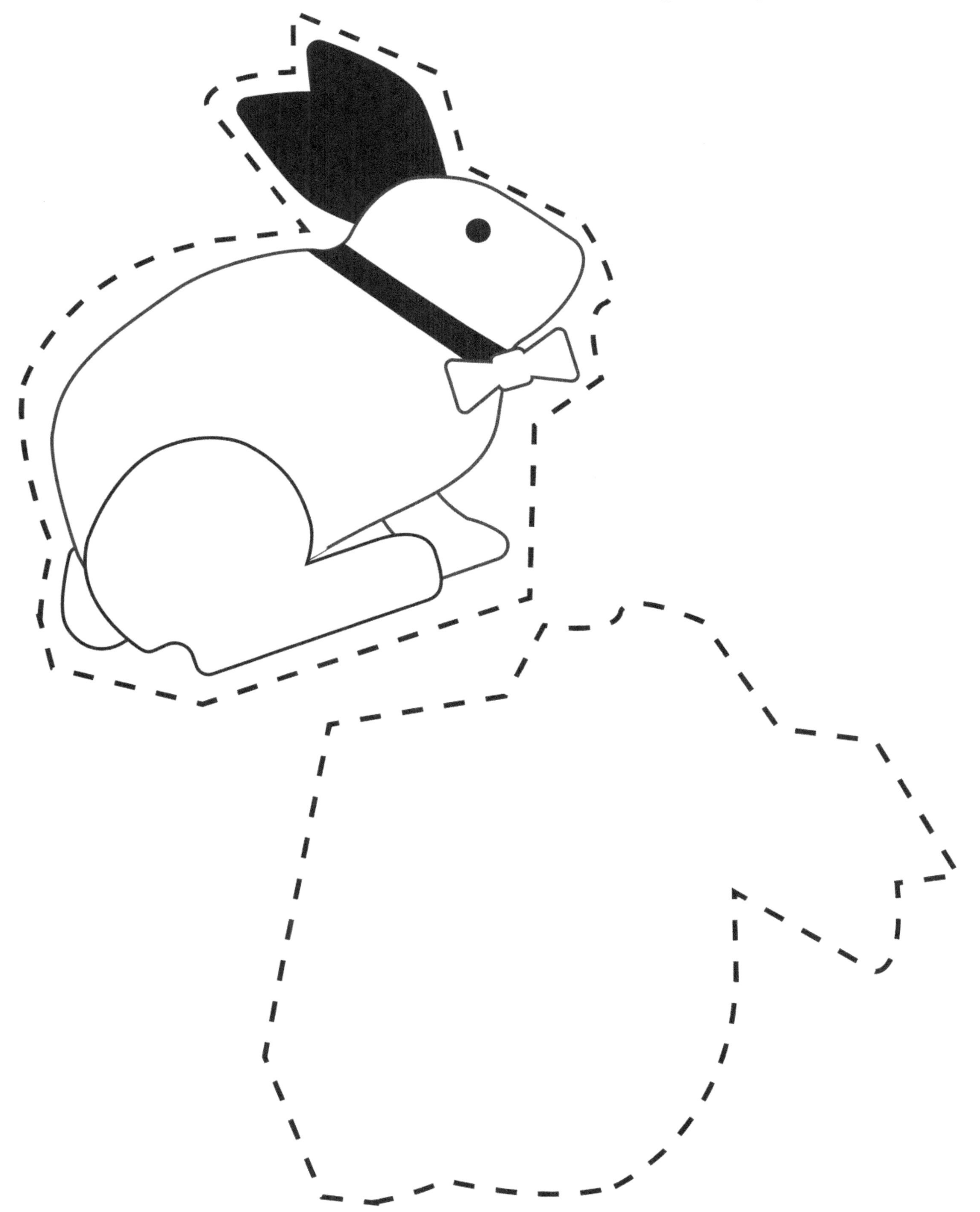

1 - Cut and the paste in the right position
2 - Color The Egg

1 - Cut and the paste in the right position
2 - Color The rabbit .

1 - Cut The Letters
2 - Place it in the right place
3 - Form the word : EASTER

1 - Cut The Letters
2 - Place it in the right place
3 - Form the word : Bunny

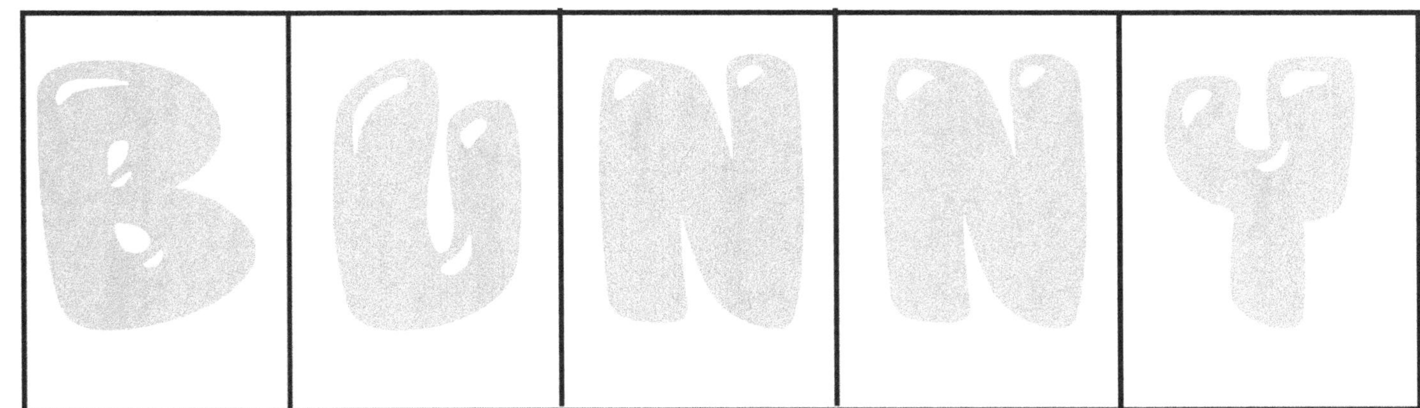

1 - Cut The Letters
2 - Place it in the right place
3 - Form the word : Egg

1 - Cut The Letters
2 - Place it in the right place
3 - Form the word : Egg

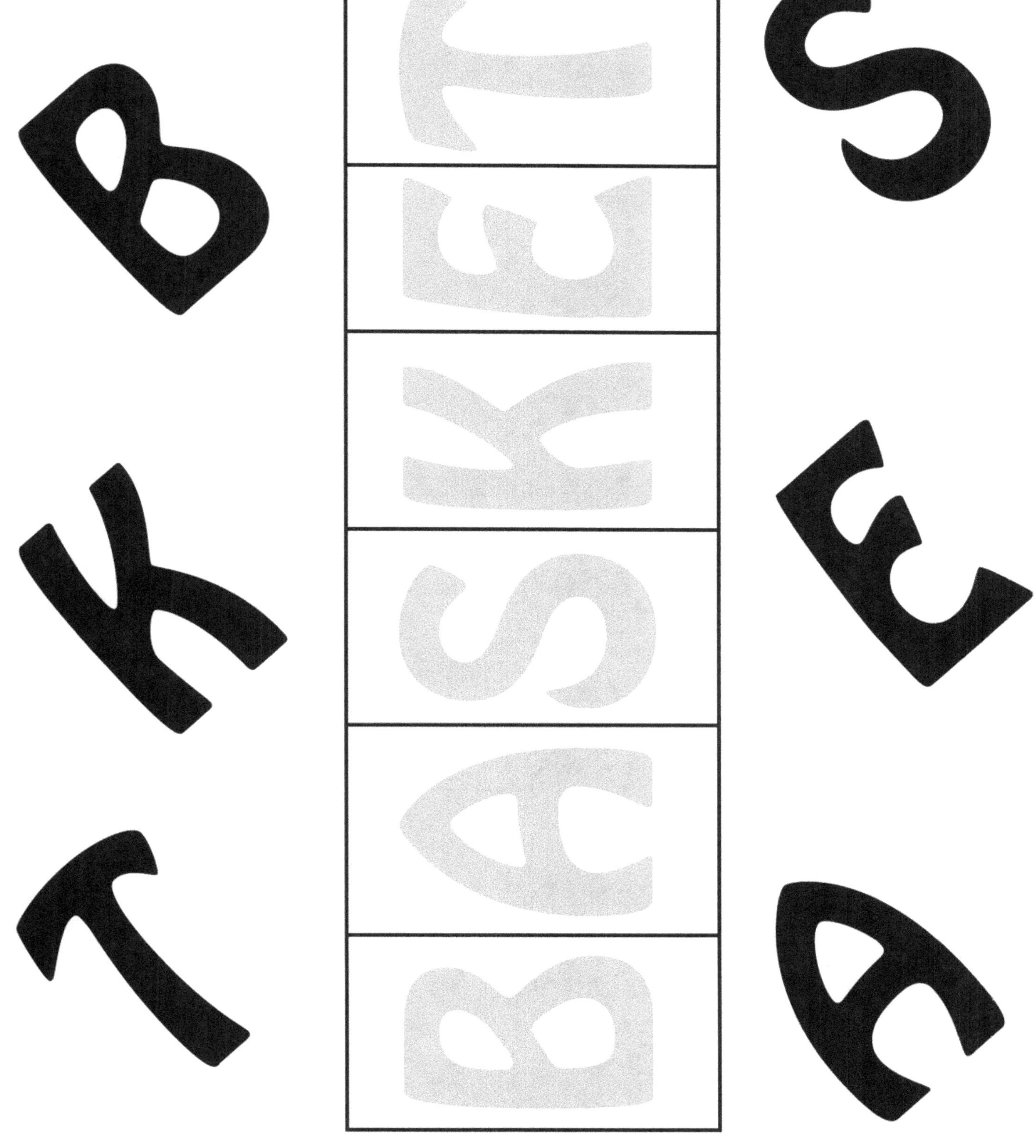

LET'S COLOR

www.ingramcontent.com/pod-product-compliance
Lightning Source LLC
Chambersburg PA
CBHW080245260726
48658CB00008B/3230